1997 Ex

Suggested Solutions

Law of Tort

LLB

University of London
External Examinations

Solutions by Michael Tookey
LLB, Barrister-at-law

HLT Publications

HLT PUBLICATIONS
200 Greyhound Road, London W14 9RY

Reprinted 2000

ISBN 0 7510 0832 X

British Library Cataloguing-in-Publication.

A CIP Catalogue record for this book is available from the British Library.

Printed and bound in Great Britain.

CONTENTS

ACKNOWLEDGEMENT

The questions used are taken from the University of London LLB (External) Degree examination paper and our thanks are extended to the University of London for the kind permission which has been given to us to use and publish the questions.

Caveat

The answers given are not approved or sanctioned by the University of London and are entirely our responsibility.

They are not intended as 'Model Answers', but rather as Suggested Solutions.

The answers have two fundamental purposes, namely:

a) To provide a detailed example of a suggested solution to examination questions, and

b) To assist students with their research into the subject and to further their understanding and appreciation of the subject.

Note

Please note that the solutions in this book were written in the year of the examination. They were appropriate solutions at the time of preparation, but students must note that certain caselaw and statutes may subsequently have changed.

INTRODUCTION

Why choose HLT publications?

Holborn College has earned an international reputation for the outstanding quality of its teaching, Textbooks, Casebooks and Suggested Solutions to past examination papers.

Our expertise is reflected in the outstanding results achieved by our students in the examinations conducted by the University of London LLB Honours Degree Programme for External Students, the Council of Legal Education, and by students in over 70 universities who use our publications.

Suggested Solutions

The Suggested Solutions series provides examples of full answers to the problems posed by examiners. The solutions are much more than answers achievable by a candidate under examination conditions. The opportunity has been taken, where appropriate, to develop themes, suggest alternatives and set out additional material providing further comprehensive topical coverage.

To aid comprehension and revision, the solutions are fuller than would be possible under examination conditions. It is important to keep in mind that at this level there almost certainly is more than just one approach in answering any given question.

We feel that in writing full opinion answers we can assist you with your research and further your understanding and appreciation of the law.

Notes on examination technique

Although the SUBSTANCE and SLANT of the answer changes according to the subject-matter of the question, the examining body and syllabus concerned, the TECHNIQUE of answering examination questions does not change.

You will not pass an examination if you do not know the substance of a course. You may pass if you do not know how to go about answering a question although this is doubtful. To do well and to guarantee success, however, it is necessary to learn the technique of answering problems properly. The following is a guide to acquiring that technique.

Time

All examinations permit only a limited time for papers to be completed. All papers require you to answer a certain number of questions in that time, and the questions, with some exceptions carry equal marks.

It follows from this that you should never spend a disproportionate amount of time on any question. When you have used up the amount of time allowed for any one question STOP and go on to the next question after an abrupt conclusion, if necessary. If you feel that you are running out of time, then complete your answer in note form. A useful way of ensuring that you do not over-run is to write down on a piece of scrap paper the time at which you should be starting each part of the paper. This can be done in the few minutes before the examination begins and it will help you to calm any nerves you may have.

Reading the question

It will not be often that you will be able to answer every question on an examination paper. Inevitably, there will be some areas in which you feel better prepared than others. You will prefer to answer the questions which deal with those areas, but you will never know how good the questions are unless you read the whole examination paper.

You should spend at least 10 MINUTES at the beginning of the examination reading the questions. Preferably, you should read them more than once. As you go through each question, make a brief note on the examination paper of any relevant cases and/or statutes that occur to you even if you think you may not answer that question: you may well be grateful for this note towards the end of the examination when you are tired and your memory begins to fail.

Re-reading the answers

Ideally, you should allow time to re-read your answers. This is rarely a pleasant process, but will ensure that you do not make any silly mistakes such as leaving out a 'not' when the negative is vital.

The structure of the answer

Almost all examination problems raise more than one legal issue that you are required to deal with. Your answer should:

Identify the issues raised by the question

This is of crucial importance and gives shape to the whole answer. It indicates to the examiner that you appreciate what he is asking you about.

This is at least as important as actually answering the questions of law raised by that issue.

The issues should be identified in the first paragraph of the answer.

Deal with those issues one by one as they arise in the course of the problem

This, of course, is the substance of the answer and where study and revision pays off.

If the answer to an issue turns on a provision of a statute, CITE that provision briefly, but do not quote it from any statute you may be permitted to bring into the examination hall
Having cited the provision, show how it is relevant to the question.

If there is no statute, or the meaning of the statute has been interpreted by the courts, CITE the relevant cases
'Citing cases' does not mean writing down the name of every case that happens to deal with the general topic with which you are concerned and then detailing all the facts you can think of.

You should cite only the most relevant cases – there may perhaps only be one. No more facts should be stated than are absolutely essential to establish the relevance of the case. If there is a relevant case, but you cannot remember its name, it is sufficient to refer to it as 'one decided case'.

Whenever a statute or case is cited, the title of statute or the name of the case should be underlined
This makes the examiner's job much easier because he can see at a glance whether the relevant material has been dealt with, and it will make him more disposed in your favour.

Having dealt with the relevant issues, summarise your conclusions in such a way that you answer the question
A question will often say at the end simply 'Advise A', or B, or C, etc. The advice will usually turn on the individual answers to a number of issues. The point made here is that the final paragraph should pull those individual answers together and actually give the advice required. For example, it may begin something like: 'The effect of the answer to the issues raised by this question is that one's advice to A is that ...'

Related to the previous paragraph, make sure at the end that you have answered the question
For example, if the question says 'Advise A', make sure that is what your answer does. If you are required to advise more than one party, make sure that you have dealt with all the parties that you are required to and no more.

Some general points

You should always try to get the examiner on your side. One method has already been mentioned – the underlining of case names, etc. There are also other ways as well.

Always write as neatly as you can. This is more easily done with ink than with a ball-point.

Avoid the use of violently coloured ink eg turquoise; this makes a paper difficult to read.

Space out your answers sensibly: leave a line between paragraphs. You can always get more paper. At the same time, try not to use so much paper that your answer book looks too formidable to mark. This is a question of personal judgment.

NEVER put in irrelevant material simply to show that you are clever. Irrelevance is not a virtue and time spent on it is time lost for other, relevant, answers.

EXAMINATION PAPER

UNIVERSITY OF LONDON
LLB EXAMINATIONS 1997
for External Students
PART I EXAMINATION (Scheme A)
SECOND AND THIRD YEAR EXAMINATIONS (Scheme B)
GRADUATE ENTRY LEVEL II (Route A)
GRADUATE ENTRY SECOND AND THIRD YEAR (Route B)

LAW OF TORT

Friday, 6 June: 10.00 am to 1.00 pm

Answer *FOUR* of the following EIGHT questions.

1 Hettie was a patient at the Manpool Hospital. Ian, the junior doctor in her ward, decided that to combat an infection she should receive a daily course of injections. In entering the details in the computer he put the decimal point in the wrong place. When Jane, the newly qualified nurse in the ward, gave Hettie her injections, she was surprised by the dosage but was too shy to question it. She therefore gave Hettie the dose shown, which was ten times that which was appropriate. Within a few hours Hettie's face, arms and legs had become extremely painful, swollen and grotesquely disfigured. Hettie's brother, Kevin, came to visit her next day. He had not been told of her appearance and was extremely shocked. Both Jane and Kevin have suffered severe psychiatric damage.

Advise Hettie, Jane and Kevin.

2 Describe, and explain the purpose of, the concept of vicarious liability. Consider what, if any, development of the concept is appropriate now that the pattern of employment is changing and many people do not work for a single permanent employer.

3 Sally, aged 10 and a very promising pianist, went to the Grungetown funfair with her mother. She took a ride on the children's chair-o'-plane. While she was on the ride, some pieces of metal broke off. Sally was struck in the arm. The ride was stopped immediately by an automatic safety mechanism and Sally was left trapped in her chair at the top of the ride. Tom, a visitor to the funfair, told staff that he was a steel erector and accustomed to working at

heights, and that he was therefore willing to climb up and attend to Sally before the emergency services arrived. Tom had almost reached Sally when he lost his footing and fell to the ground. Sally was released after half an hour, but her arm was permanently disabled. Tom broke his back in the fall and is permanently paralysed and unable to find work.

Advise Sally and Tom as to their entitlement to damages and the principles on which any damages are assessed.

4 Cruella Enterprises Ltd manufacture leather garments. They receive a threat from an 'animal rights' organisation that their factory will be occupied by protesters. This is reported to the managing director who decides that it is a hoax and takes no special security measures. Two weeks later a bomb explodes beside a drum of acid which the company uses in its manufacturing processes. The acid pours into the adjoining premises of DeVile Ltd where a large number of used car tyres are stored. Thousands of pounds worth of damage is done to the tyres and the reaction with the acid unexpectedly produces toxic vapours. Neighbouring factories have to close down for several days until the vapours have dispersed.

Advise Cruella Enterprises and DeVile.

5 Discuss the following cases:

a) A supermarket chain sells many lines under its own brand name 'Salmonella'. Peggy buys a packet, labelled 'Salmonella sliced apples. Produce of England. Vacuum packed. Suitable for home freezing. Freeze immediately on purchase. Eat within three months.' Peggy puts them in her home freezer as soon as she gets home two hours after she has purchased them. She uses them two months later. She and her daughter Queenie suffer severe food poisoning which is traced to the apple slices.

b) Ruth buys in England some marker pens manufactured by Ecoli GmbH in Germany. Her teenage son Simon uses the red and white pens to paint a St George's Cross on his face before he joins the spectators at an international soccer match. The red pen contains a pigment which causes a severe rash and itching on Simon's face, which persists for several months.

6 Evaluate the changes made by the Defamation Act 1996. Are there any other changes to the law of defamation which you would like to see?

7 Theta invented a new computer game which he hoped would prove attractive in the lucrative Christmas trade for 1996. In May he approached Alphaline in the hope that they would be willing to market it in the United Kingdom. Alphaline showed considerable interest. Theta was however concerned about the financial stability of Alphaline and asked to see a copy of their most recent accounts. These had been prepared by Kappa. In the light of these accounts Theta decided that it would be too risky to give Alphaline the exclusive right to market the game. He then approached

Betaline. Betaline commissioned a report from Sigma. Sigma sent Betaline an appraisal headed 'Confidential. For your information only.' It reported that the underlying concept of the game was too complicated and that it would have only very limited appeal. Betaline therefore refused to act for Theta. Disheartened Theta did not pursue the matter further.

Alphaline is still a flourishing company in June 1997, the accounts prepared by Kappa presented an unduly gloomy picture. A game with a very similar concept to Theta's was developed in the United States and was extremely successful in the British market at Christmas 1996.

Advise Theta.

8 Fred is driving his sister Gail to the railway station on a dark evening so that she can catch an overnight train to Scotland for an important meeting. They have been held up in heavy traffic and Gail is convinced that she will be late. After they have waited at a red light for some time, Gail exclaims, 'You stupid fool. The lights have jammed. There's not a thing in sight. Get a move on.' Fred can see no traffic approaching and moves across the junction. He strikes a bicycle ridden at a fast speed by Harry, who is wearing black jeans and sweater. Gail is injured. Harry has unusually brittle bones and dies of his injuries.

Advise Gail and Harry's estate.

SUGGESTED SOLUTIONS

QUESTION 1

Hettie was a patient at the Manpool Hospital. Ian, the junior doctor in her ward, decided that to combat an infection she should receive a daily course of injections. In entering the details in the computer he put the decimal point in the wrong place. When Jane, the newly qualified nurse in the ward, gave Hettie her injections, she was surprised by the dosage but was too shy to question it. She therefore gave Hettie the dose shown, which was ten times that which was appropriate. Within a few hours Hettie's face, arms and legs had become extremely painful, swollen and grotesquely disfigured. Hettie's brother, Kevin, came to visit her next day. He had not been told of her appearance and was extremely shocked. Both Jane and Kevin have suffered severe psychiatric damage.

Advise Hettie, Jane and Kevin.

SUGGESTED SOLUTION TO QUESTION 1

General Comment

This question requires a consideration of breach of duty and, in particular, the 'reasonable man' standard applicable to medical professionals. The effect of lack of experience, and the distinction between prognosis and treatment, should be discussed, as should the vicarious liability of the hospital authority. The question of nervous shock/psychiatric injury should be given reasonable prominence; in particular the sibling relationship and the time-scale/causative aspects.

Skeleton Solution

Duty; breach of duty; the 'reasonable man' standard.

The *Bolam* test; prognosis and treatment; the duties owed by Ian and Jane.

Inexperience and the need to acquire expertise.

Nervous shock; primary and secondary victims.

Siblings as secondary victims/'mere bystanders'.

The time gap and causation.

Vicarious liability of the hospital.

Suggested Solution

There is overwhelming authority for the proposition that a medical professional or a health authority will owe a duty of care to patients undergoing treatment; the necessary foreseeability, proximity and 'just, fair and reasonable' aspects of a duty are patently present. The real question is of the standard of care required to discharge the duty or, conversely, below which a breach of duty occurs. The case law has put a gloss upon a 'reasonable man' objective standard so that the test to apply to medical professionals is that of McNair J in *Bolam* v *Friern Hospital Management Committee* (1), that of 'the ordinary skilled man exercising and professing to have that special skill'. This test has found great favour with the English courts and has been held to apply not simply to medical professionals but to other types of professional and, indeed, to any situation where one is exercising skill and expertise: see *Bolitho* v *City and Hackney Health Authority* (2).

We are not told whether Ian has discussed the proposed injections with Hettie or not. This raises the point whether any failure to consult Hettie or to advise her about possible effects would, in itself, constitute negligence. *Sidaway* v *Board of Governors of the Bethlem Royal* (3) shows that the same test should apply to giving advice about proposed treatment as to the standard required in giving treatment, ie the *Bolam* test. Ian will be measured against this. On balance, in failing to spot a very significant error in time, he would be likely to be found to have fallen below the standards of any body of reasonably competent medical professionals and, as a consequence, to have breached his duty towards Hettie. The question of any duty owed to Kevin is dealt with below.

The same *Bolam* reasoning will apply to Jane as a nurse. The question might be raised as to whether the standard should be lowered to allow for her relative inexperience (or, indeed, that of Ian). This will not be a factor; this much is clear from *Wilsher* v *Essex Area Health Authority* (4). There is no room for a sliding scale varying with experience.

The damage to both Jane and Kevin is psychological in nature and this can create problems because of restrictive judicial attitudes towards recovery for this type of damage. The first question is whether the sufferer is categorised as a primary victim, ie one who suffers psychiatric damage as a result of a sudden shock to the system caused by the negligence of the tortfeasor. Here, there is little problem for Hettie's recovery because there are no special restrictive mechanisms at work, and recovery is based upon simple *Donoghue* v *Stevenson* (5) principles as in *Dulieu* v *White* (6) and *Page* v *Smith* (7). The test is one of reasonable foreseeability of any type of physical (including mental) damage to such victims. By contrast, where a sufferer is a secondary victim, ie one who suffers shock because of danger or harm caused to another by the negligence of the tortfeasor, the special restrictions imposed by *McLoughlin* v *O'Brian* (8), as explained and extended by *Alcock* v *Chief Constable of South Yorkshire* (9), come into play.

There are two problems raised by these cases in the situation in question. The first one is the categorisation of the victims. Hettie is arguably a primary victim, although we are not told of the precise means or process by which her condition arose. There would be no difficulties for her in the light of *Page* v *Smith* in that, provided some harm to her person was foreseeable, the precise type need not be foreseeable. Kevin can only, on the given facts, be a secondary victim. According to the House of Lords, such a victim must stand in such a relationship to the person harmed or in danger as would exhibit the sort of ties of love and affection to be found between spouses or between parents and children. This is a question of fact in the particular circumstance, according to *Alcock*. If the relationship is not this close, Kevin is likely to be equated with a 'mere bystander' and unable to recover: *McFarlane* v *E E Caledonia* (10).

Jane is in a rather anomalous position. She is possibly to be considered as a 'mere bystander' but it is more likely that her damage results from her knowledge of involvement in Hettie's injury. She would find assistance from her employee status as equating to a 'professional rescuer' within *Frost* v *Chief Constable of South Yorkshire* (11) and possibly from *Dooley* v *Cammell Laird & Co* (12).

The second problem raised by the House of Lords cases is that of the closeness in time and space between the negligence giving rise to shock-causing event and the time at which the secondary victim observes the result and is shocked. Where there is no subsequent negligence by the original tortfeasor, the passage of time beyond the 'immediate aftermath' tends to bar recovery as in *Alcock*; there are too many possibilities for novus actus interveniens. Here, there seems to be no such problem because the fact of permitting visitors (or any unprepared person) to see such a shocking sight is, arguably, a quite separate act of negligence in itself. There might be defence arguments of novus actus interveniens, if, for example, Kevin had sought Hettie out without notifying anyone of his presence.

The hospital, as employers of Ian and Jane, will almost certainly be vicariously liable for such torts as they have committed within the course of their employment. There is nothing here to suggest that they were acting otherwise than in the course of employment. If the hospital system was at fault in allowing Kevin to visit Hettie unprepared, its liability will be primary.

References

(1) [1957] 1 WLR 582
(2) (1997) The Times 27 November
(3) [1985] AC 871
(4) [1988] AC 1074
(5) [1932] AC 562
(6) [1901] 2 KB 669
(7) [1995] 2 All ER 736
(8) [1983] AC 410
(9) [1991] 3 WLR 1057
(10) [1994] 2 All ER 1
(11) [1996] NLJ 1651
(12) [1951] 1 Lloyd's Rep 271

QUESTION 2

Describe, and explain the purpose of, the concept of vicarious liability. Consider what, if any, development of the concept is appropriate now that the pattern of employment is changing and many people do not work for a single permanent employer.

SUGGESTED SOLUTION TO QUESTION 2

General Comment

In such a question, the narrative and descriptive of parts of the question should be dealt with fairly shortly. The essential points, such as necessary relationships and course of employment, judicial controls, etc, should be covered, but the candidate should take a vigorous approach to the real problems and possible solutions that follow from rapidly changing patterns of occupation. Consideration of alternative safeguards, such as statutory schemes, insurance, etc, might be discussed.

Skeleton Solution

The origins and nature of vicarious liability.

The significance of employment situations as distinct from independent contractor situations.

The social and economic arguments involved.

Changes in working patterns and the implications for vicarious liability.

Suggested changes and developments to the doctrine; legislative intervention and insurance arrangements.

Suggested Solution

The modern doctrine of vicarious liability has its historical roots in the idea that the master should be liable for the torts of his servant, if committed 'within the course of employment'. This pattern of liability to third parties within a close and well-known relationship has remained to modern times, and vicarious liability will still arise only in such relationships as employer/employee or principal/agent. There remains also the requirement that the tort should be committed within the course of employment or, with agents, within some express or implied or ostensible authority: *Storey* v *Ashton* (1) (employees); *Lloyd* v *Grace, Smith & Co* (2) (agency). The question of just what distinguishes an employee from some other form of contractor has occupied the courts to a very considerable extent and, after several attempts at a satisfactory rationale, such as the 'control test' (*Yewens* v *Noakes* (3)) and the 'in business on own account' test from *Market Investigations Ltd* v *Minister of Social Security* (4) (still used for taxation purposes), the modern view seems to prefer the three-stage approach favoured by MacKenna J in *Ready Mixed Concrete (South East) Ltd* v

Minister of Pensions (5) as being more appropriate to the question of vicarious liability for torts.

The question of 'course of employment' can be seen from the cases as being one that the courts consider a matter for decision by them rather than one which is dictated by the employer and the terms of employment. This is highlighted by cases on the effect of express prohibitions, such as the contrasting cases of *Twine* v *Bean's Express Ltd* (6) and *Rose* v *Plenty* (7). It is clear that the court will be the final arbiter of what is an 'unauthorised act' so as to take the matter outside the course of employment, preferring, on occasion, to find that the matter is an 'unauthorised mode of doing an authorised act' as in *Limpus* v *London General Omnibus Co Ltd* (8).

A finding that an employment relationship subsists is usually much more advantageous to the third party victim of a tort because the alternative, that the tortfeasor is an independent contractor, means that the general vicarious liability of the employer for torts within the course of employment is replaced by an altogether narrower range of liabilities under which one independent contractor is, by way of exception to the general rule, liable for torts committed by an independent contractor employed by him. If the tort falls outside this narrower band of exceptional situations, the victim will only have a remedy against the direct tortfeasor who may sometimes be unable to satisfy a judgment.

The legal rationale for vicarious liability seems, at bottom, to come down to a matter of 'social convenience and rough justice': per Lord Pearce in *Imperial Chemical Industries Ltd* v *Shatwell* (9). It seems logical that liability should fall jointly upon the primary tortfeasor and the person best able to profit from the other's labours and who, as employer, is in an infinitely better position to obtain insurance cover at sensible rates; the employer will be the one best able to assess the range of risk, scale of damage and the quality of employee required for the employment.

The doctrine of vicarious liability arose over a period in which the distinction between employee and self-employed was obvious and clear. Over the last few decades, patterns of business and occupation have changed to an unprecedented degree, with a large part of the adult working population becoming increasingly involved in part-time and short-period engagements. In combination with the business attractiveness of reducing employed labour forces this has led to many situations where the true working relationship is often extremely unclear. Examples of this can be seen in the *Ready Mixed Concrete* and *Market Investigations* cases. In many cases, the very reason for these changes is to restrict the liabilities to others, including third parties. Clearly, as matters stand, this will reduce the possibilities for vicarious liability, especially where the use of individual independent contractors replaces an employee workforce. This has gone hand-in-hand with a perceived increase in the use of the so-called 'masters indemnity' against the tortfeasor employee as seen in *Lister* v *Romford Ice and Cold Storage Co Ltd* (10), probably at the instance of the insurers.

Is there, then, anything that can be done to help the third party in such circumstances? A possibility might be to extend the liability for the torts of independent contractors to the situation where, if the damage to a third party were reasonably foreseeable had it been caused by an employee, the fact that an independent contractor is used will not prevent a joint liability arising. This might be combined with a statutorily implied term into any such contract that, in the event that the parties had not agreed upon which party provides third-party cover, the liability will be deemed to be joint. In any event, the matter would require legislation; short of this, matters will have to progress naturally and only time will show how useful vicarious liability will be in the future.

References

(1) (1869) LR 4 QB 476
(2) [1912] AC 716
(3) (1880) 6 QBD 530
(4) [1969] 2 QB 173
(5) [1968] 2 QB 497
(6) [1946] 1 All ER 202
(7) [1976] 1 WLR 141
(8) (1862) 1 H & C 526
(9) [1965] AC 656
(10) [1957] 1 All ER 125

QUESTION 3

Sally, aged 10 and a very promising pianist, went to the Grungetown funfair with her mother. She took a ride on the children's chair-o'-plane. While she was on the ride, some pieces of metal broke off. Sally was struck in the arm. The ride was stopped immediately by an automatic safety mechanism and Sally was left trapped in her chair at the top of the ride. Tom, a visitor to the funfair, told staff that he was a steel erector and accustomed to working at heights, and that he was therefore willing to climb up and attend to Sally before the emergency services arrived. Tom had almost reached Sally when he lost his footing and fell to the ground. Sally was released after half an hour, but her arm was permanently disabled. Tom broke his back in the fall and is permanently paralysed and unable to find work.

Advise Sally and Tom as to their entitlement to damages and the principles on which any damages are assessed.

SUGGESTED SOLUTION TO QUESTION 3

General Comment

This question raises a wide range of issues so the planning of the answers is vital. Some attempt must be made to deal with Sally's cause(s) of action arising from the original impact and the delay in reaching safety and receiving attention; and the causative effects of the safety mechanism as well as the legal basis and extent of her recovery should be discussed. As for Tom, it will be necessary to consider his position both as visitor and as rescuer, possible defences based upon volenti non fit injuria and contributory negligence, and the basis and extent of his recovery.

Skeleton Solution

Sally's possible causes of action: negligence, under Occupiers' Liability Act 1957; *Rylands* v *Fletcher*; breach of statutory duty.

The automatic safety device; the half-hour delay; possible multiple causation and possible novus actus interveniens.

Sally's basis of recovery; loss of amenity and her musical prospects; remoteness of damage.

Tom as visitor: possible defences.

Tom as rescuer: possible defences.

Tom's basis of recovery.

Suggested Solution

We are not told the precise cause of the metal fracture. The evidence on this may affect the causes of action relied upon by Sally, but the various possibilities that suggest themselves are: negligence simplicitor based on a failure to maintain or inspect; breach of the common duty of care owed to lawful visitors by the funfair as occupiers under the Occupiers' Liability Act (OLA) 1957; and there might be an 'escape' within the meaning attached to that phrase under the principle in *Rylands* v *Fletcher* (1); there might, indeed, be a breach of statutory duty involved as a great deal of fairground machinery is affected by such duties, particularly where safety fencing of moving machinery is involved.

To examine possible difficulties within such a range of potential causes of action is not possible in the time available so, for present purposes, it is assumed that the damage was reasonably foreseeable and that Sally will have a good cause of action based on common law negligence and under the OLA

1957. The next question is whether Sally's injury was in any way affected by the half-hour delay caused by the automatic safety mechanism. If there is no particular additional damage caused by the delay, the situation between Sally and the funfair remains unchanged; if there was reasonable foreseeability of the metal fracture there was also likely to be reasonable foreseeability of the delay in reaching the ground. If, by contrast, the delay has caused some identifiable increase in damage, such as might occur with splintered bones or severed nerves, there is a possible defence argument that the automatic safety system has interfered with the causative process as a possible novus actus interveniens. This would be a complex argument and would probably turn on the question of how foreseeable the consequence was, and how practicable it was to get emergency access and egress. If there were real problems with causation, the court would adopt a commonsense approach: *Yorkshire Dale Steamship Co Ltd* v *Minister of War Transport* (2).

Sally's recovery for her personal injuries will be along conventional lines, in that she would receive special damages for provable losses to the date of trial, such as damaged clothes, wasted school fees or tuition fees, extra travelling costs, etc. She will also recover for general damages under several heads. She would be able to recover for pecuniary loss in respect of future loss of earning potential, which would be likely to be estimated on an annual percentage sum below the national adult average earnings at the time of trial (the 'multiplicand') multiplied by a number of 'years purchase' representing her working lifetime (the 'multiplier'), which would be considerably reduced to allow for 'accelerated receipt'. The effect of taxation and national insurance contributions on earnings would be allowed for: *British Transport Commission* v *Gourley* (3). Any additional prospective expenses, such as adaptation of home or chattels, might be claimed for, as well as prospective medical expenses. Sally will also, under general damages, recover for pain, suffering and loss of amenity in line with similar injury awards as evidenced by works such as Kemp and Kemp, but there may be a very considerable argument as to whether she will be able to recover for the devastating loss of amenity in being unable to pursue her musical interests and, possibly, a career. The speculative aspects of much of this with a plaintiff aged tenmay well restrict recovery to something nearer to what a healthy non-musician might have recovered. Much will turn on the evidence as to her promise as a musician; the process is analogous to remoteness of damage considerations.

Tom might claim as a visitor under the OLA 1957, on the basis that the funfair staff permitted him to attempt a rescue. He may well fare better under this if there is any defence claim of unnecessary rescue or volenti than if he claims under common law as a rescuer. The fairground will be unable to raise the 'special risks, ordinary incident' defence in s2(3)(b) OLA 1957 because he is not exercising his calling but, instead, is there as their permitted rescuer, although they may raise a volenti non fit injuria defence against him under s2(5). If volenti is raised, the same principles will apply as if Tom proceeded as a rescuer of Sally on ordinary negligence grounds. He is unlikely to be seen as volenti (*Baker* v *T E Hopkins and Sons Ltd* (4)) unless the rescue was seen to be 'wanton' as in *Cutler* v *United Dairies Ltd* (5).

Tom's basis of recovery is similar to that of Sally, except that his loss of earning capacity will be much easier quantified, and there will be heavy existing and prospective costs for attendance and nursing care, again worked out on a multiplicand / multiplier basis.

References

(1) (1868) LR 3 HL 330
(2) [1942] AC 691
(3) [1956] AC 185
(4) [1959] 1 WLR 966
(5) [1933] 2 KB 297

QUESTION 4

Cruella Enterprises Ltd manufacture leather garments. They receive a threat from an 'animal rights' organisation that their factory will be occupied by protesters. This is reported to the managing director who decides that it is a hoax and takes no special security measures. Two weeks later a bomb explodes beside a drum of acid which the company uses in its manufacturing processes. The acid pours into the adjoining premises of DeVile Ltd where a large number of used car tyres are stored. Thousands of pounds worth of damage is done to the tyres and the reaction with the acid unexpectedly produces toxic vapours. Neighbouring factories have to close down for several days until the vapours have dispersed.

Advise Cruella Enterprises and DeVile.

SUGGESTED SOLUTION TO QUESTION 4

General Comment

Students should be prepared to deal with the general question of whether a duty exists to prevent the acts of third parties and how far such a duty might extend. The question also requires a consideration of the law of nuisance and *Ryland* v *Fletcher*. The nature of the damage will also require some discussion of unlikely or remote consequences, and pure and consequential economic loss. The vicarious liability of the company for the torts of its managing director should be discussed.

Skeleton Solution

Whether there is a duty to prevent the acts of third parties: *Smith* v *Littlewoods*.

The claim by DeVile Ltd: negligence, nuisance and *Rylands* v *Fletcher*.

The claims brought by the neighbouring factories against Cruella Enterprises Ltd, and DeVile Ltd.

The unexpected consequences; *Cambridge Water* v *Eastern Counties Leather*; remoteness of damage.

The range of recovery; consequential economic loss; pure economic loss.

Vicarious liability.

Suggested Solution

The original source of the damage in this situation is the unlawful bombing of Cruella's factory and, if it were possible to find the miscreants, they could be held to account. But, as this result is unlikely, Cruella will be probably forced back upon their insurers for their own property damage. The real question is to what extent, if at all, will Cruella be liable for damage to others. The complaint that will be levelled against the company and its managing director is that they failed to prevent the act of the 'animal rights' third party. This directly raises the question whether, and in what circumstances, such a duty arises. The leading case is now *Smith* v *Littlewoods Organisation Ltd* (1), from which it is clear that no such operational duty exists but that within certain exceptional situations, Lord Goff illustrating four, a duty may arise.

In Cruella's situation, some of the exceptional features may be present. Lord Goff pointed to the case where a landowner allows or knows that a source of danger on his land is being created by a third party as a situation where a duty might arise; similarly, a duty may arise where a person has created or tolerated a potential danger which only needs the agency of a third party to 'trigger off' a risk to others as in *Haynes* v *Harwood* (2). It is assumed for present purposes that such a duty is owed by Cruella and, in the absence of evidence of how secure the site and acid storage is under normal circumstances, that the duty is breached. This duty will be owed, at least, to adjoining owners such as DeVile Ltd under conventional 'neighbour' principles: per Lord Atkin in *Donoghue* v *Stevenson* (3).

The claim by DeVile Ltd may, as outlined above, be brought on ordinary negligence principles. If, however, it were found that Cruella's security was such that no special measures were needed or, perhaps, practicable, this cause of action would disappear. It would then be necessary to consider alternatives, and the ones that suggest themselves are nuisance and / or *Rylands* v *Fletcher* (4) liability. A claim might be brought in private nuisance, even for an isolated escape, if there is evidence of a generally insecure site with an underlying, unsatisfactory state of affairs as in *British Celanese* v *A H Hunt Ltd* (5), but this sort of claim would fail in the circumstance of a reasonably secure site and storage as with the claim in negligence. It might, however, succeed if the overall site security was good (preventing a negligence claim) but the storage of acid left something to be desired. A more promising probability would be under *Rylands* v *Fletcher* on the basis that Cruella had brought a substance onto their premises which was likely to do harm if it escaped. This use of their land would, undoubtedly, be a 'non-natural' use and this is the very type of situation for which the remedy is intended. The acid has simply escaped under gravity, but there is a defence to *Rylands*, that of the act of a stranger as in *Perry* v *Kendrick Transport Ltd* (6). However, as Cruella knew that there was a possibility of sabotage, this might not be a defence here. Liability under *Rylands* v *Fletcher* depends very much upon reasonable foreseeability, both of the escape and of the consequences of the escape: *Cambridge Water* v *Eastern Counties Leather plc* (7).

The neighbouring factories, if they claim against Cruella, may have some difficulties whatever cause of action they rely upon. The problem is that the rules of remoteness of damage laid down in *The Wagon Mound (No 1)* (8) show that property damage of a type that is not reasonably foreseeable is unrecoverable. This would seem to bar a negligence action based on toxic vapours, and a very similar result obtains in nuisance and *Rylands* v *Fletcher* since the *Cambridge Water* case. This would not, of course, prevent a claim by DeVile Ltd against Cruella for direct acid damage to the tyres.

An even more formidable obstacle for the neighbouring factories is that most of their loss appears to be in the form of lost production. There are two possibilities here. First, that there may be stock or material which has been damaged or rendered useless by the closures and, second, that the loss is pure economic loss in the form of lost productivity and continuing overhead costs. If the factories can get a claim going against Cruella (perhaps on the basis that the vapours are of the general acidic nature), they may be able to recover for the first head of the loss as that can be seen to be consequential economic loss.

They will be unable to recover for the pure economic loss in negligence or *Rylands*: *Spartan Steels and Alloys Ltd* v *Martin & Co (Contractors) Ltd* (9). The question whether such a loss is recoverable in nuisance is unclear but, as the interference is with the enjoyment of land as manufactures, there seems no reason in principle why such loss should not be recoverable.

There would be little doubt that any negligence by the managing director would be 'within the course of his employment' so as to bring down vicarious liability on Cruella.

There is the possibility that the neighbouring factories may wish to claim against DeVile for the escape of fumes from their premises under *Rylands* v *Fletcher*. This could probably be met by a defence of lack of reasonable foreseeability under *Cambridge Water* v *Eastern Counties Leather plc* or possibly act of a stranger as in *Perry* v *Kendrick Transport Ltd*.

References

(1) [1987] AC 241
(2) [1935] 1 KB 146
(3) [1932] AC 562
(4) (1868) LR 3 HL 330
(5) [1969] 1 WLR 959
(6) [1956] 1 WLR 85
(7) [1994] 2 WLR 53
(8) [1961] AC 388
(9) [1973] QB 27

QUESTION 5

Discuss the following cases:

a) A supermarket chain sells many lines under its own brand name 'Salmonella'. Peggy buys a packet, labelled 'Salmonella sliced apples. Produce of England. Vacuum packed. Suitable for home freezing. Freeze immediately on purchase. Eat within three months.' Peggy puts them in her home freezer as soon as she gets home two hours after she has purchased them. She uses them two months later. She and her daughter Queenie suffer severe food poisoning which is traced to the apple slices.

b) Ruth buys in England some marker pens manufactured by Ecoli GmbH in Germany. Her teenage son Simon uses the red and white pens to paint a St George's Cross on his face before he joins the spectators at an international soccer match. The red pen contains a pigment which causes a severe rash and itching on Simon's face, which persists for several months.

SUGGESTED SOLUTION TO QUESTION 5

General Comment

The question is clearly concerned with processed or manufactured products which have caused personal injury to persons who could be described as 'consumers'. Some analysis of the terms of the Consumer Protection Act (CPA) 1987 is called for and, perhaps, some comment on the improved situation under the CPA 1987 as against the common law.

Skeleton Solution

Scope of the Act and incidence of liability, type of product.

Producers, suppliers and liability to person supplied and others.

Nature of the damage and 'defects'; range of recoverable damage.

Defences.

Suggested Solution

a) Peggy and Queenie have both suffered personal injury as a result of eating apple slices which, by reason of having been machine sliced and packaged, could be said to be a 'product'. This is very important because it brings the matter within the general sphere of product liability as compared with untreated, unprocessed, agricultural produce which is governed by an altogether looser regime imposed by the law of sale of goods and the common law. The Consumer Protection Act (CPA) 1987 provides a very comprehensive and effective type of strict liability where damage has been caused by a 'defect' in a product in a 'consumer' situation. Section 2(4) implies that agricultural produce which has 'undergone an industrial process' is within the ambit of the Act.

The incidence of liability is set out in s2(2) and (3) and it clearly attaches to the 'producer' (s2(2)(a)) and others who hold themselves, by brand or mark, out as the producer (s2(2)(b)), thus catching the supermarket chain. The chain will also be caught as a 'supplier' within s2(3) regardless of the fact that they did not supply the goods direct to Queenie. This express inclusion of suppliers goes a long way towards remedying the severe limitations on the liability of suppliers which were imposed by the common law and only partly remedied by the 'manufacturer's role' in *Donoghue* v *Stevenson* (1).

Section 2(3) also shows that the basis of liability is damage 'caused wholly or partly by a defect in a product'. Clearly, there is no room for foreseeability here and the damage, once causation has been established, is strict so it is obvious that one great drawback with the foreseeability-based common law approach has been removed; the problem from *Evans* v *Triplex Safety Glass Co Ltd* (2) has disappeared. A 'defect' is defined by s3(1) as meaning that 'the safety of the product is not such as persons generally are entitled to expect', with s3(2) going on to highlight particular circumstances which need to be taken into account in considering what 'persons generally are entitled to expect'.

The instructions on the package (s3(2)(a)) may be adequate, but it is a question of fact whether there is enough information about the need to maintain the vacuum or otherwise for the safety of the consumer. Apart from that, there is the possibility that a two-hour delay, particularly if temperatures were high during the two hours, might have affected matters. But a one- to two-hour delay ought, perhaps, to be anticipated by a producer. In all other respects, the food has been used in accordance with the instructions and there are strong indications of a defect. The range of recoverable damages clearly contemplates personal injury (ss3(1) and 5(3)), but not loss in respect of the product itself (s5(2)), and the liability cannot be ousted by disclaimers, notice etc (s7).

The liability is strict, but not absolute, so the statutory defences within s4 must be considered. The vitally important point about s4 is that the legal burden of proof of the defence is placed upon the defendant producer/supplier by s4(1). The only defence that seems able to be run by the defendant in this case is that in s4(1)(d), ie 'that the object did not exist in the product at the relevant time', the relevant time here being the time of supply. This will be a heavy burden for the chain to discharge in the circumstances.

b) The marker pen is clearly a 'product' and the incidence of liability will apply to the 'producer', Ecoli GmbH (s2(2)(a)). This provision is likely to apply to the UK supplier if it fails, on request for information about the manufacturer by Simon as the person who suffers damage, to supply details (s2(3)(b)). If the supplier were liable, the liability of producer and supplier would be joint and several. As outlined above, the supply to a person other than the damaged person does not matter provided that there was a supply 'to another' (s4(1)(b)) and that it was a normal business supply (s4(1)(c)).

There could be some real difficulties in establishing that there is a 'defect' within s3 in that it is highly likely that the marker pens carried some sort of warning against using on skin. If they did not, there is likely to be an argument that there should be a warning unless Simon has a highly sensitive skin. The express requirement under s3(2)(b) to consider 'what might reasonably be expected to be done with or in relation to the product' would seem to indicate against there being a defect.

The type of damage is within the range of the Act, but if the evidence showed that appropriate medical testing had failed to indicate such a reaction, ie Simon was hypersensitive, the 'development risks' defence within s4(1)(e) might well be relied upon. The Act seems to be working very well in that there is almost a complete absence of case law on the 'defects' provisions, so closer analysis of high-sensitivity complainants must necessarily await judicial examination of the Act.

Neither (a) nor (b) above seem to fall outside the Act so it is not necessary to consider the residual common law jurisdiction which will now mainly apply to non-consumer situations.

References

(1) [1932] AC 562
(2) [1936] 1 All ER 283

QUESTION 6

Evaluate the changes made by the Defamation Act 1996. Are there any other changes to the law of defamation which you would like to see?

SUGGESTED SOLUTION TO QUESTION 6

General Comment

This question requires the student to highlight the perceived improvements upon the former position, rather than an arid description of the provisions of the 1996 Act. Some emphasis is needed on the summary procedures provided and, if possible, some comment on the 1991 Neill Report. There is scope in this question to deal with the perceived problems that the Act does not really address in detail, such as jury damages awards, 'internet' defamations, exemplary damages etc.

Skeleton Solution

Section 1: innocent dissemination.
Sections 2–4: unintentional defamation and offers of amends.
Section 5: limitation periods.
Sections 8–10: summary disposals.
Section 13: parliamentary waivers.
Damages awards by juries.
New techniques of publication.
Exemplary damages.

Suggested Solution

The Defamation Act 1996 has introduced a wide-ranging series of reforms to the existing law, both by way of clarification and substantive reform. Only time and use will show how effective the legislation is, but any assistance at all in this complex area is welcome. The 1996 Act came about as a result of widespread dissatisfaction with the existing law which led to a Lord Chancellor's Consultation Paper in 1990 and the recommendations of Lord Justice Neal in his 1991 Report, many of which are reflected in the Act.

Section 1 has codified the former common law defence of innocent dissemination and, very helpfully, has defined the scope of the defence by exclusion of 'authors', 'editors' and 'publishers', going on in s1(2) to further define the excluded class, and in s1(3) the included class. As at common law, it will be for the defendant to show that he took 'reasonable care' in respect of a publication and that he did not know, and had no reason to believe, that he was publishing a defamation. This is unlikely to prove too onerous a burden for anyone other than a defendant who habitually operates close to the limit.

Sections 2–4 bring in a greatly improved regime for an unintentional defamation defence of apology and offer of amends. This is quite different from the former regime under s4 Defamaton Act 1952 in that it contemplates that, in the event of failure to agree on either the steps to be taken by way of correction, apology and publication or the amount of compensation in amends, both matters will be determined by the court. This will only be appropriate in the circumstance where the sum offered, or likely to be decided upon, is less than £10,000 because that is the current upper limit for summary disposal by the judge alone (s9(1)).

There are other important changes in ss2–4 in that a defendant who intends to rely upon apology and amends as a defence must do so before he puts forward any other defence – it cannot be put forward after service of any other defence (s2(5)) – and once committed to, apology and amends cannot, thereafter, rely upon other defences (s4(4)). The defendant can, however, use an offer to try to mitigate damages whether he has relied on it for a defence or not (s4(5)). An extremely important change is brought in by s4(3) which raises a statutory presumption that the defendant was innocent of the knowledge of reference to the plaintiff and of the defamatory effect upon the plaintiff. This completely reverses the burden of proof on this vital matter and is likely, by itself, to lead to a great increase in using this provision as against its predecessor, s4 Defamation Act 1952.

Section 5 adds new ss4A and 32A to the Limitation Act 1980 so as to reduce limitation periods for defamation and malicious falsehood to one year as against the former three years and six years, subject to a judicial discretion to extend the period on equitable grounds which are wider than the former rules on accrual of knowledge of a right to an action.

Sections 8 to 10 make very sweeping changes in that they allow a judge to take full control of actions where the plaintiff has no realistic prospects of success and there is no other reason to try the claim or an application by the plaintiff for summary disposal, or where matters under ss2–4 are in dispute. In all cases, the disposal is by the single judge and the overall range of matters suitable for summary trial is capped at £10,000 damages. Otherwise than on a plaintiff's insistence the judge will not act summarily unless he is satisfied that summary relief will adequately compensate the plaintiff (s8(3)). This begins to bring defamation proceedings at the lower end of the scale more in line with other types of action, and the intention seems to be that, ultimately, all claims of whatever scale will come before the judge at an interlocutory stage for consideration of the possibility that a summary disposal is possible.

Section 13 brings in, for the first time, a possibility for waiver of the absolute privilege attaching to parliamentary proceedings by persons covered by the privilege so that they may conduct defamation proceedings. This came about as a result of the 'cash for parliamentary questions' issues and is likely to be but sparingly relied upon, although its potential value can be seen.

The Act might have gone further in attempting to deal with the vagaries of awards of damages by juries, perhaps by giving the judge a discretion to remit questionable awards directly to the Court of Appeal for consideration under s8 Courts and Legal Services Act 1990. Time will tell how much such a change is still required or, indeed, whether jury awards should be replaced by the decision of the judges. It may be that the bubble of such awards has been burst by the guidelines in *John* v *MGN Ltd* (1).

The Act might, similarly, have gone further in response to information technology developments, although s1(3) has arguably touched on the problem of computerised defamations. Also, the immense sums of money to be gained from deliberate defamations with profit in view might well have provided a reason to expand upon the circumstances in which exemplary damage awards might be made. Perhaps the legislators have retained their confidence in the common law and its ability to cope with such matters. The Act has, at least, moved forward on some fronts.

Reference

(1) [1996] 2 All ER 35

QUESTION 7

Theta invented a new computer game which he hoped would prove attractive in the lucrative Christmas trade for 1996. In May he approached Alphaline in the hope that they would be willing to market it in the United Kingdom. Alphaline showed considerable interest. Theta was however concerned about the financial stability of Alphaline and asked to see a copy of their most recent accounts. These had been prepared by Kappa. In the light of these accounts Theta decided that it would be too risky to give Alphaline the exclusive right to market the game. He then approached Betaline. Betaline commissioned a report from Sigma. Sigma sent Betaline an appraisal headed 'Confidential. For your information only.' It reported that the underlying concept of the game was too complicated and that it would have only very limited appeal. Betaline therefore refused to act for Theta. Disheartened Theta did not pursue the matter further.

Alphaline is still a flourishing company in June 1997, the accounts prepared by Kappa presented an unduly gloomy picture. A game with a very similar concept to Theta's was developed in the United States and was extremely successful in the British market at Christmas 1996.

Advise Theta.

SUGGESTED SOLUTION TO QUESTION 7

General Comment

In this situation, the nature of the loss indicates that Theta will be required to look at the area of *Hedley Byrne* liability as extended to the recent House of Lords cases. There are always problems with prospective lost profits recovery in negligence, and in Betaline's situation the problem is further complicated by the context of a specially commissioned report which indicates a contractual relationship. There are also considerable problems of causation and remoteness which should be examined.

Skeleton Solution

Theta and Kappa accounts: the purpose of preparation and the scope of any duty owed; proximity.

Theta and the Sigma report; lack of proximity.

Theta and Betaline: whether Betaline advised Theta and whether there was justifiable reliance.

Theta/Betaline and Sigma: the contractual context; concurrent tort/contract liability; the heading to the appraisal; proximity.

The product developed in America: causation and remoteness.

Suggested Solution

It is assumed, for present purposes, that Kappa and Sigma had been negligent in preparing the accounts and the appraisal, respectively. The accounts prepared by Kappa were, presumably, prepared for Alphaline only and there seems to be no reason why Kappa should have had Theta in mind when they prepared them. This is an important point because Theta is considering a potential loss of profits which can only be characterised as prospective pure economic loss. The only cause of action which suggests itself is negligent misstatement within the principle in *Hedley Byrne & Co Ltd* v *Heller & Partners Ltd* (1). Because the scope for actions based on negligent words is potentially so wide the courts have insisted on a fairly narrow rule of proximity between the parties as in *Caparo Industries plc* v *Dickman* (2). This would indicate that Kappa's duty of care would be unlikely to extend beyond Alphaline and its members, although had Kappa been asked or told about the further communication to Theta, a duty might then arise. Even if there were a duty,

Theta would have severe problems in proving the nature and extent of his reliance and the causation of his damage in such circumstances.

Theta then is further frustrated in his plans by Betaline's refusal to act for him. It appears that Theta probably knew nothing of the Sigma report so it will be difficult for him to claim that he relied upon it to his detriment. If this is the case, any claim based upon negligent misstatement falls at the first hurdle because reliance is the whole basis of this area of obligation and there cannot be reliance without knowledge.

There is a possibility that Betaline may have gone further than a simple refusal to act and might have indicated their reasons. These are marketing specialists and there is a possibility that some liability might attach to loose words used by them if it is reasonably foreseeable that Theta might rely upon them. There is no need for the defendant to have specialised knowledge (*Howard Marine and Dredging Co* v *A Ogden and Sons (Excavations) Ltd* (3)), but the more specialised a person is, and the less sophisticated the recipient of the statement, the more likely it is that a duty may arise: *Smith* v *Eric S Bush* (4). There would, however, be a serious difficulty for Theta to overcome here. Betaline have indicated that they themselves will not proceed with Theta, but there are no indications that they have gone so far as to positively advise him against further investigation of marketing potential. Without this it seems unlikely that a claim will lie; a simple loss of enthusiasm after a rebuff would not be the sort of reliance exhibited in the case law. This would apply particularly where the advice took the shape of a refusal to enter a commercial arrangement.

Betaline have almost certainly entered into a contractual relationship in commissioning an appraisal from Sigma. There is a possibility that Sigma may feel that they are advising both partners to a prospective joint venture. This is a question of evidence and, if this is the case, Theta would almost certainly be able to pursue Sigma for breach of implied term in contract, absent a clear disclaimer. If Sigma had disclaimed, the possibility of a tort action remains but the courts are reluctant to allow a circumvention of the contract in this way (*Tai Hing Cotton Mill* v *Liu Chong Hing Bank* (5)), although there is no doubt now that concurment liability in tort and contract can exist: *Henderson* v *Merrett Syndicates Ltd* (6).

If Sigma are clear that they are only advising Betaline, the heading to their appraisal seems to make clear an intention that the matters referred to should not be passed on to another, which should be enough to prevent a duty arising to persons other than Betaline. The use of the word 'information' may indicate that they seek to disclaim any liability for reliance along the lines seen in *Royal Bank Trust Co (Trinidad) Ltd* v *Pampellone* (7), where a distinction was drawn between 'information' and 'advice'.

Any claim at all by Theta will meet great difficulties in quantifying the loss because of the great success of the American product on the British market in 1996. This raises complex arguments of causation in the sense of whether there would have been a market for Theta's product and of remoteness as to the extent of a potential market position for the future. Theta has very great problems in establishing any claim at all.

References

(1) [1964] AC 465
(2) [1990] 2 AC 605
(3) [1978] QB 574
(4) [1990] 1 AC 831
(5) [1986] AC 80
(6) [1994] 3 WLR 761
(7) [1987] 1 Lloyd's Rep 218

QUESTION 8

Fred is driving his sister Gail to the railway station on a dark evening so that she can catch an overnight train to Scotland for an important meeting. They have been held up in heavy traffic and Gail is convinced that she will be late. After they have waited at a red light for some time, Gail exclaims, 'You stupid fool. The lights have jammed. There's not a thing in sight. Get a move on.' Fred can see no traffic approaching and moves across the junction. He strikes a bicycle ridden at a fast speed by Harry, who is wearing black jeans and sweater. Gail is injured. Harry has unusually brittle bones and dies of his injuries.

Advise Gail and Harry's estate.

SUGGESTED SOLUTION TO QUESTION 8

General Comment

This type of question calls for an exposition of the various defences to negligence, as well as some discussion of joint liability and the extent of the remedies involved. With so many points to cover, some degree of economy on detail is needed, and planning of the answers is particularly important.

Skeleton Solution

Duty; breach; joint liability to Harry; contribution.

Gail's claim against Fred; defences – volenti, contributory negligence, ex turpi causa.

Harry's claim; defences.

Remoteness and the brittle bones.

The claim by the estate.

Suggested Solution

The duty owed by one road user to another is so well established as to be beyond question. The real issues here are whether Gail will owe any duty towards Harry in addition to Fred, who obviously will, and whether there has been breach. Breach may be assumed because, even if the lights had broken down, it would have been prudent for Gail to get out of the car to have better visibility of other road users, but this would normally only show breach by Fred, as the driver. There is an argument here that Fred is acting in the furtherance of a common design in crossing the lights and this may be enough to bring down joint liability upon Gail for Fred's negligence as in *Brooke* v *Bool* (1).

Alternatively, there may be an argument that Fred is acting as agent to Gail as principal and has committed a tort within his express authority, thus making her vicariously liable along the lines seen in *Ormrod* v *Crossville Motor Services Co Ltd* (2). If this is the situation there would be nothing to prevent Fred's insurers (or the Motor Insurers Bureau if he were uninsured) seeking contribution against her under s1 Civil Liability (Contribution) Act 1978. A similar joint liability arose in *Scarsbrook* v *Mason* (3), although the House of Lords in *Morgans* v *Launchbury* (4) warned against too easy a recourse to agency principles in car cases where there was generally no fault on the part of the 'principal'. Here there seems to be primary fault on Gail's part.

Gail will be seeking recovery for her own injuries, probably against Fred and his insurers. Various defences may suggest themselves. Although the circumstances indicate that the absolute defence of volenti non fit injuria is in point, this defence is barred by s149(3) Road Traffic Act 1988 as against a passenger. This would not, of course, prevent a defence claim that Gail had contributed to her injuries by want of care for her own safety, and that the damages that she might be awarded should be reduced to reflect a just apportionment of her own blameworthiness under s1(1) Law Reform (Contributory Negligence) Act 1945. There might be a defence claim that, as the pair had agreed to do what is a criminal offence by the driver, her claim should be met by the defence of ex turpi causa non oritur actio. There is no doubt that injuries to, and torts against, the participants in illegal joint enterprises may sometimes be defended by ex turpi causa, but recent cases such as *Revill* v *Newbery* (5) and *Pitts* v *Hunt* (6) show that a very restrictive view is taken of this defence, particularly where illegality is simply in the mode of driving a vehicle.

As to Harry's claim, there may be a possibility of defences of volenti and contributory negligence. We are not told whether Harry had lights on his bicycle but, assuming that he did not, this might support a claim that he was contributorily negligent. He seems to have been travelling quickly which might be adding to an impression of want of care. In *Tremayne* v *Hill* (7) a pedestrian, who failed to watch out for cars going through traffic lights on red, was held not to be contributorily negligent, but it is by no means certain that the same result would follow where a cyclist is going quickly, without lights, in dark clothes at night. All that needs to be established for contributory negligence is a want of care for one's own safety: *Nance* v *British Columbia Electric Railway Co Ltd* (8). There seems little chance of establishing a volenti defence against Harry's claim because there must be some evidence that Harry was aware of the danger which was 'extreme and glaring' and, nevertheless, resolved to undertake the risk of it as in *Morris* v *Murray* (9). There is nothing equivalent to that here except as referred to below.

It may be that had Harry not had such brittle bones, he might have survived the incident, possibly with minor injuries. In the normal run of matters, a defendant cannot be heard to raise such a defence because the governing principle is that the tortfeasor must 'take his victim as he finds him', ie with his weaknesses (*Dulieu* v *White and Sons* (10)), and this principle extends liability to unexpected types of personal injury as in *Smith* v *Leech, Brain and Co* (11), as well as to greater than expected degrees of damage. This must, of course, give way to the argument that if a person knows that he is extremely vulnerable to certain types of injury, this will, in a proper case, increase the possibility of a contributory negligence defence and, in a very extreme situation, the possible argument that he was volenti to an obvious, extreme and glaring risk.

The claim by Harry's estate will be brought under s1 Law Reform (Miscellaneous Provisions) Act 1934 on the same basis that he himself, had he survived, would have claimed for his personal injuries and damage to his bicycle, clothes, etc. The estate would not be able to claim for his 'lost years' earnings, but would be able to claim for funeral expenses (s1(2)(c)). The claim for his personal injuries would be along conventional lines and much would depend upon what pain, suffering and loss of amenity he suffered prior to his death, as well as lost earnings up to that time. Had Harry any surviving dependants, those persons could bring an action under the Fatal Accidents Act 1976 for bereavement, funeral expenses and actual and future pecuniary losses based upon the valuation of the lost dependency when taken over the period that such a dependency was likely to last. The basis of the calculation for a wage earner is usually the earnings up to the accident less whatever part which was spent by the deceased on his own upkeep. A suitable multiplier is then worked out by reference to the projected length of the dependency, and a suitable discount applied for accelerated receipt of the award, but this claim is for the benefit of the dependants and does not go to the estate.

References

(1) [1928] 2 KB 578
(2) [1953] 1 WLR 1120
(3) [1961] 3 All ER 767
(4) [1973] AC 127
(5) [1996] 2 WLR 239
(6) [1991] 1 QB 24
(7) [1987] RTR 131
(8) [1951] AC 601
(9) [1991] 2 WLR 195
(10) [1901] 2 KB 669
(11) [1962] 2 QB 405

